This Is Our World

by Barbara L. Luciano

Editorial Offices: Glenview, Illinois • Parsippany, New Jersey • New York, New York
Sales Offices: Needham, Massachusetts • Duluth, Georgia • Glenview, Illinois
Coppell, Texas • Sacramento, California • Mesa, Arizona

This is the world.

We need to keep it safe.

We need to keep it clean.

We need to save resources.

We can recycle.

What can you do?

Glossary

recycle to turn materials into new materials

resources things we need

world where we live